Plan, Prepare, COOK

A Tasty Dinner

A+

Smart Apple Media

Contents

Published by Smart Apple Media,
an imprint of Black Rabbit Books
P.O. Box 3263, Mankato, Minnesota 56002
www.blackrabbitbooks.com

U.S. publication copyright © 2015 Smart Apple
Media. International copyright reserved in all
countries. No part of this book may be reproduced
in any form without written permission from the
publisher.

Printed in the United States by Worzalla,
Stevens Point, Wisconsin.
PO1655
4-2014

Published by arrangement with the
Watts Publishing Group LTD, London.

Library of Congress Cataloging-in-Publication Data

Storey, Rita.
 A tasty dinner / Rita Storey.
    pages cm -- (Plan, prepare, cook)
 Audience: Grades 4 to 6.
 Includes index.

ISBN 978-1-59920-955-5
1. Cooking--Juvenile literature. 2. Dinners and
dining--Juvenile literature. I. Title.
 TX652.5.S695 2015
 641.5'4--dc23

                                    2013034428

Picture credits
All photographs Tudor Photography, Banbury
unless otherwise stated. Shutterstock p5;
Wishlistimages.co.uk p4

Cover images Tudor Photography
All photos posed by models. Thanks to Jack Abbott,
Amy Mobley, Serish Begum, and Jordan
McElavaine.

Free activity sheets are available for pages marked with ⬇. Request them at info@blackrabbitbooks.com. Find out more on page 32.

Words in **bold** are in the glossary on page 30.

Before You Start

- Wash your hands before and after preparing food.
- Ask an adult to help when the recipe uses the oven or stovetop.
- If you have long hair, clip or tie it back.
- Dry your hands before you plug in or unplug any electrical appliances.
- Wear an apron or an old shirt.
- Wash up as you go along.
- Be extra careful with sharp knives.
- Ask an adult to help with the blender or food processor.
- Ask an adult to help you measure the ingredients.

Look for this useful guide to each recipe.

How long each recipe takes to make.

How difficult each recipe is to make.

Whether the food needs to be cooked.

All about Dinner

For most people dinner is the main meal of the day and is eaten in the evening.

Fast Food

Supermarkets and restaurants sell a wide variety of ready-prepared meals. This "fast food" may be high in sugar and **fat**. It also often contains artificial **colorings** and **flavorings**, as well as **preservatives**.

Starchy Foods

You should eat **starchy** foods every day—they should make up about a third of what you eat in a day. A portion of potatoes, pasta, or rice is a good idea as part of dinner.
- Choose **whole grain** or **whole wheat** varieties.

Meat, Fish, Chicken, Eggs, and Beans

These foods contain **protein**. Meat, fish, and eggs are often the basis of dinner. Beans also contain protein, and they can replace meat or fish for **vegetarians**.

Try not to eat this type of **processed food** too often.

If you are in a hurry, cooking a bowl of pasta with a delicious sauce can be just as fast as heating up a ready-prepared meal. It will taste great and is healthy too.

The recipes in this book are quick and easy. Knowing that you have prepared and cooked them yourself is really satisfying.

Why We Eat

The human body is like a machine that needs **energy** to work. Energy is released from the food you eat and used up by your body.

A Healthy Balance

To be healthy, you must eat enough food to produce the energy needed by your body. But if you eat more food than your body actually requires, it is turned into fat. If you do this all the time, you keep getting fatter.

When you **exercise,** you use up energy from the food you have eaten.

Fruit and Vegetables

You should eat at least five portions of fruit and vegetables every day (5-a-day). A portion of fruit or vegetables is about ½ cup (80 g.), or roughly one handful. Fruit and vegetables should make up about a third of what you eat in a day. Frozen, canned, and dried fruits and vegetables all count. Try to eat lots of different types. Add a portion or two of your favorite vegetables to your dinner.

Exercise burns up energy and can be a lot of fun!

Milk, Cheese, and Yogurt

Cheese is made from milk. It contains protein.

These cheeses have a creamy texture: cream cheese, ricotta, mozzarella

Soft cheese has a soft, sticky texture: Brie, Camembert

Hard cheese can be grated: Cheddar, Parmesan

Beware—some cheeses contain a lot of fat.

sugar, so it is a good idea to read the information on the package carefully.

Choose whole grain or whole wheat pasta and rice. They have lots of **vitamins**, **minerals,** and **fiber**. They also taste great.

Food Labels

Some foods are better for you than others. Foods that are high in salt, sugar, or fat are not healthy if you eat them too often. Foods that are labeled "low-fat" can sometimes contain a lot of

Look at the labels on food to find out which are high in salt, sugar, and fat.

Shopping and Planning

Planning, preparing, and cooking food for yourself, friends, and family is fun, and you get to eat well too!

Think of something you would like to make for dinner. Write a shopping list of the things you need.

Check with the people you are cooking for to find out if there are any foods they dislike. Some people do not eat meat or fish. They are called vegetarians.

Before you start cooking, read through the recipe and collect all the ingredients and equipment together.

Cooking

Read the instructions carefully before you start. Ask an adult to explain anything that you do not understand.

A tidy kitchen is much easier to work in than a messy one. Clean up and put things away as you work.

Wash the dishes and wipe down work surfaces as you prepare and cook the food.

Chicken Dippers

These tasty chicken nuggets are perfect to eat with a sweet and spicy dip and crunchy salad.

You Will Need

- measuring spoons
- bowl
- plate
- baking sheet
- oven mitts
- small dish and serving plate

Ingredients

- 1 tablespoon oil
- 2 tablespoons stuffing mix
- 2 tablespoons flour
- 2 tablespoons grated Cheddar cheese (see page 29)
- 8 oz (225 g.) chicken mini fillets or sliced chicken breast
- 2 tablespoons sweet chili sauce
- 4 tablespoons mayonnaise
- cherry tomatoes, sticks of cucumber and peppers

This makes enough for 2 people.

Before You Start

- Preheat the oven to 400° F (200° C).

- Measure the oil into a bowl.

- Put the stuffing mix, flour, and grated cheese onto a plate.
- Mix together.

- Dip one of the chicken pieces in the oil until it is covered all over.

4

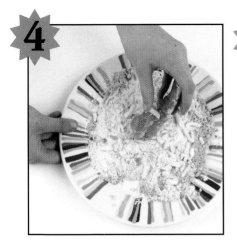

- Roll the chicken piece in the flour, cheese, and stuffing mix.

5

- Place the chicken piece on the baking sheet. Repeat stages 3 and 4 with the rest of the chicken pieces.

6

- **Bake** in the oven for 15 to 20 minutes.
- Using the oven mitts, take out the baking sheet.
- Ask an adult to check that the chicken is cooked properly.
- Turn off the oven.

7

- Mix the sweet chili sauce and mayonnaise in a bowl.

Serve some dipping sauce in a dish with the chicken pieces, cucumber, peppers, and tomatoes around it.

Get Dipping!

45 minutes

Medium

Cooked

Cheese "Surprise" Burgers

These tasty burgers are made with the cheese in the middle. Bite into them for a cheesy surprise.

You Will Need

- large mixing bowl
- wooden spoon
- small mixing bowl
- fork
- cutting board
- small knife

Ingredients

- 8 oz (225 g.) ground beef
- 1 egg
- 2 oz (50 g.) Cheddar cheese
- 1 onion, peeled and chopped
- 2 teaspoons dried mixed herbs
- a pinch of salt
- salad to serve with the burgers (see pages 14–15)

This makes 4 burgers.

Before You Start

- Turn the **broiler** on to high.

1

- Put the ground beef in the large mixing bowl. Break up any lumps with a wooden spoon.

2

- Crack the egg (see page 28) into the small mixing bowl and whisk with a fork.

3

- Cut the cheese into four pieces.

4

- Put the egg, onion, and mixed herbs into the bowl with the meat. Add the salt, and mix everything together.
- Place the mixture on the cutting board.

5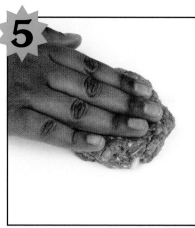

- Divide the mixture into four pieces, and shape each piece into a ball.
- Flatten each ball with your hand to make your burgers.

6

- Put a piece of cheese in the middle of each burger.
- Wrap the meat around the cheese. There should not be any cheese showing.

7

- Put the burgers on a broiler pan. Broil for about 8 minutes on each side.
- Ask an adult to check that the burgers are cooked properly.
- Turn off the broiler.

Serve each burger with a delicious salad.

Mmmmm

| 30 minutes |
| Medium |
| Cooked |

Stuffed Potato Skins

Potatoes make a filling base for dinner. Use these fillings or experiment with some of your own.

Ingredients

- 2 medium baking potatoes (washed)
- 1 tablespoon vegetable oil
- small can of tuna fish (drained)
- 2 tablespoons sour cream
- 2 tablespoons corn
- 2 green onions, finely chopped
- 2 tablespoons grated Cheddar cheese

You Will Need

- baking sheet
- fork
- pastry brush
- sharp knife
- measuring spoons
- mixing bowl
- potato masher

Before You Start

- Preheat the oven to 375° F (190° C).

1

- Put the potatoes on the baking sheet. Prick the potatoes all over with a fork.
- Brush with the oil.
- Bake for an hour or until they are soft.
- Turn off the oven.

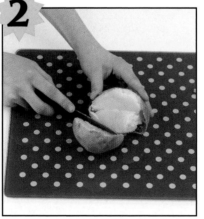

2

- Let them cool slightly. Then cut the potatoes in half.

- Scoop the soft potato into the mixing bowl. (Be careful not to break the skins.)
- Mash the potato (see page 29).

- Mix the tuna fish, sour cream, and corn with the potato.

- Spoon the mixture back into the skins.
- Top each potato with a few chopped green onions.

- Put the potatoes back into the (cooled) baking sheet.
- Top each one with a quarter of the grated cheese.
- Put into the oven until the cheese is melted and golden brown.
- Turn off the oven.

Delicious

Suggestion

Instead of a baking potato, use a large sweet potato. Mix the sweet potato with a tablespoon of sour cream and a quarter teaspoon of nutmeg. Top with grated cheese.

1 1/2 hours

Medium

Cooked

13

Filling Salads

Choose chunky potato, pasta, or rice. Add some extras from the list below and make your perfect salad.

Ingredients

Salad Base
Either:
- 2-3 (8 oz) small new potatoes
- 2 tablespoons mayonnaise

Or
- 1 cup (115 g.) uncooked pasta
- 2 tablespoons mayonnaise

Or
- ½ cup (115 g.) brown rice
- salad dressing (see Handy Hint)

Plus Anything From This List:
- sausages—cooked and sliced
- ham—cooked and cut into small pieces
- tuna fish—drained and broken up
- chicken—cooked and cut into small pieces
- shrimp—cooked
- canned corn—drained
- peas—cooked
- green beans—cooked and chopped
- salmon—cooked and flaked
- broccoli, cooked and cut into small pieces

You Will Need
- saucepan
- colander or strainer
- cutting board
- knife
- bowl
- mixing spoon

Potatoes
- Put them in a saucepan. Cover them in water and bring to a boil. Cook for 20 to 30 minutes. Turn off the burner.
- Drain in a colander.
- Leave to cool.
- Cut into halves, or quarters if they are large.

Handy Hint!

To make a creamy salad dressing, mix a tablespoon of sour cream with a few chopped chives and a squirt of lemon juice.

Rice

- Put the rice in a saucepan. Cover it with water and bring to a boil. Cook for 20 to 30 minutes. Turn off the burner.
- Ask an adult to drain the rice into the strainer (over a sink).
- Let cool.

Pasta

- Put the pasta in a saucepan. Cover it in water and bring to a boil. Cook for the time stated on the package. Turn off the burner.
- Ask an adult to drain the pasta in a colander (over a sink).
- Let cool.

- **Either** mix the potato or pasta with the mayonnaise **or** mix the rice with the salad dressing.

- Add your choice of extra ingredients and mix together.

Sausage and Shrimp Pasta Salad

Mixed Vegetable Potato Salad

Salmon and Vegetable Rice Salad

| 40 minutes |
| Easy |
| Cooked |

Macaroni and Cheese

Creamy macaroni and cheese is always a favorite. Add a portion of green vegetables for a healthy, balanced meal.

Pasta

Pasta is a starchy food (see page 4). It gives you energy. Whole wheat pasta is made from wheat that has not had the outer bran layer removed to make it white. As well as having more flavor, whole wheat pasta contains more vitamins, minerals, and fiber than white pasta.

Ingredients

- 2 tablespoons butter
- 1 tablespoon flour
- 1 cup (300 ml) milk
- ½ cup (50 g.) grated Cheddar cheese
- 1 cup (100 g.) dry macaroni, cooked and drained
- vegetables and crusty bread

You Will Need

- saucepan
- wooden spoon
- measuring cups
- whisk
- mixing spoon
- baking dish

Before You Start

- Turn the burner on to medium.

1

- Melt the butter in the saucepan.

2

- Add the flour and milk.

3

- Whisk everything together until it is thick and smooth.

4

- Add half the cheese. Whisk again until smooth.

5

- Mix the sauce and cooked macaroni together.

6

- Pour the macaroni and sauce into a baking dish.
- Top with the rest of the grated cheese.
- Turn the broiler on.

7

- Put the dish under the broiler for a few minutes until the cheese is melted and golden brown.
- Turn off the broiler.

Serve with the vegetables and some crusty bread.

Cheesylicious!

| 40 minutes |
| Medium |
| Cooked |

Cheesy Beans

Beans on toast make an easy and filling snack meal. Add some cheese and a portion of mushrooms to make it even more delicious.

Ingredients

- 1 medium-sized mushroom
- 1 teaspoon cooking oil
- portion baked beans
- 1 slice whole wheat bread, toasted and buttered
- grated cheese

You Will Need

- small saucepan
- spoon
- small sharp knife
- cutting board
- small frying pan
- spatula
- serving spoon
- plate

Beans

Baked beans are a starchy food that contains fiber and protein. They are a good source of protein for people who do not eat meat. Three heaped tablespoons of beans also count as one of your 5-a-day.

Before You Start

- Turn the burner on to low.

1

- Slice the mushroom.

2

- Put the oil into the frying pan. Add the mushroom slices and cook until they are soft.
- Turn off the burner.

- Empty the beans into the saucepan.
- Put on the burner and heat gently.
- Turn off the burner once the beans are hot.

- Spoon the mushrooms on to the buttered toast.

- Top with the beans.

- Finish with a sprinkle of grated cheese.

Yummmmm

15 minutes

Easy

Cooked

Creamy Salmon
and Vegetable Pasta

This creamy pasta dinner dish is as quick to make as any instant meal. It is tasty and healthy, too.

You Will Need

- frying pan
- spatula
- plate
- large saucepan
- strainer or colander
- grater
- fork
- mixing spoon

Fish

A healthy diet includes at least two portions of fish a week, including one of **oily fish**.

Oily fish—salmon, mackerel, sardines, trout, and herring

White fish—haddock, flounder, pollack, and cod

Shellfish—shrimp, mussels, and lobster

Ingredients

- 2 tablespoons butter
- 2 salmon fillets
- 4½ oz (125 g.) fresh pasta
- 1 lemon
- 1 cup (115 g.) green vegetables, cooked and cut into pieces
- 2 tablespoons sour cream

This makes enough for 2 people.

1

- Turn the burner on to a medium heat and melt the butter in the frying saucepan.

2

- Add the fish and cook for 4 minutes.
- Using the spatula, turn it over and cook for another 4 minutes.

- Take the fish out and put it onto a plate.
- Turn the burner to high.
- Half fill the large saucepan with water and put it on the burner.

- When the water is hot, add the pasta. Bring the water to a boil and cook for 4 minutes.
- Ask an adult to drain the pasta into the strainer or colander (over a sink).

- Put the drained pasta back in the saucepan.
- Turn the burner down to low.
- Grate the yellow skin (rind) from the lemon into the saucepan.

- Break the fish into small pieces with a fork. Add the fish to the saucepan.

- Add the cooked vegetables and sour cream.
- Put the saucepan back on the burner and heat very gently for a minute or two.
- Turn off the burner.

Wow!

15 minutes

Medium

Cooked

Sticky Chicken

These sticky chicken drumsticks are coated with a barbecue-flavored sauce. They are a perfect summer picnic dish.

You Will Need

- tablespoon
- saucepan
- wooden spoon
- baking sheet
- oven mitts
- tin foil

Ingredients

- 4 chicken drumsticks

For the sauce:

- 1 tablespoon sunflower oil or olive oil
- 2 tablespoons tomato ketchup
- 1 tablespoon soy sauce
- 1 tablespoon clear honey

To serve:

- 2 portions rice salad made with peas, green beans, and corn (see page 15)

This makes enough for 2 people.

Before You Start

- Turn the burner to medium.
- Turn the oven to 400° F (200° C).

- Measure all the sauce ingredients into the saucepan.

- Put the pan on the burner.
- Melt the ingredients together. Stir with a wooden spoon. When they are mixed, turn off the burner.

- Put the chicken drumsticks on a baking sheet.
- Pour the sauce over them.

- Bake in the oven for 15 minutes.
- Using the oven mitts, take out the tray. Spoon the sauce back over the chicken.
- Put the drumsticks back in the oven and bake for another 15 minutes.
- Ask an adult to check that the chicken is cooked properly.
- Wrap foil round the ends of the drumsticks to make them easier to pick up.
- Turn off the oven.

Serve with a rice salad (see page 15).

Stickylicious!

| 40 minutes |
| Medium |
| Cooked |

Marvelous Meringues

These "light as a feather" meringues are very easy to make and melt in your mouth.

Ingredients
- 2 eggs, separated (see page 28)
- ⅔ cup (115 g.) **superfine sugar** or graulated sugar
- heavy cream, whipped (see page 29)
- raspberries

You Will Need
- large mixing bowl
- electric mixer
- baking sheet
- spoon
- kitchen knife

Handy Hint!

It is very important not to get any yolk in the egg white when you separate the eggs. If you do, the egg whites will not thicken.

1

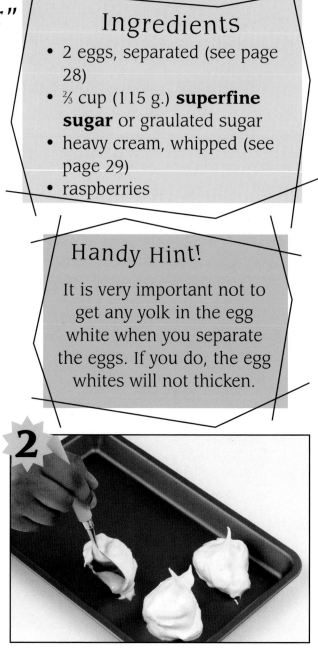

- Put the egg whites into a bowl.
- Beat with the electric mixer on high until the whites are very thick. To check, turn off the mixer. Lift it up, out of the mixture. The egg whites should stand up in stiff points.
- Beat in the sugar a little at a time.

2

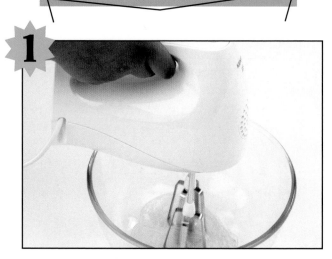

- Put spoonfuls of the mixture on to a baking sheet.
- Turn the oven to 250° F (120° C).
- **Bake** the meringues for 1½ to 2 hours. They should be firm and dry to touch.

- Turn off the oven and leave the meringues to cool.
- When they are cold, spread the bases with a blob of whipped cream.

- Sandwich the meringues together.
- Decorate with raspberries.

Yummmm

2-3 hours

Tricky

Cooked

Special Fruit Kebabs

These fruit kebabs with a chocolate coating are a great way to add to your 5-a-day (see page 5).

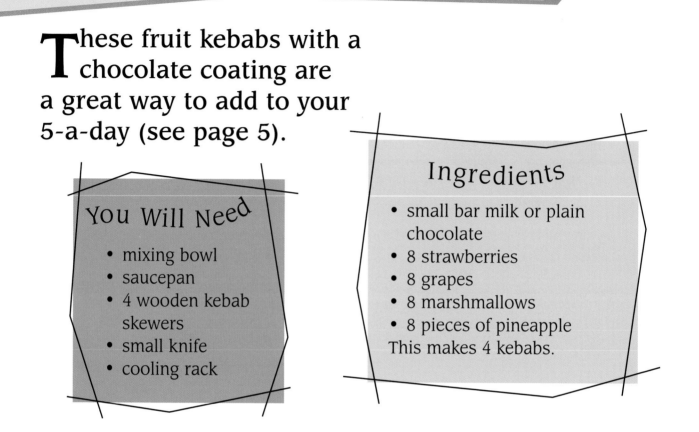

You Will Need

- mixing bowl
- saucepan
- 4 wooden kebab skewers
- small knife
- cooling rack

Ingredients

- small bar milk or plain chocolate
- 8 strawberries
- 8 grapes
- 8 marshmallows
- 8 pieces of pineapple

This makes 4 kebabs.

1

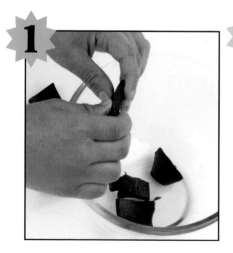

- Break the chocolate into the mixing bowl.
- Turn the burner on to medium.

2

- Put some water in the pan. Rest the bowl on top of the pan. The water should not touch the bottom of the bowl.

- Put the pan on the burner. Stir occasionally as the chocolate melts.

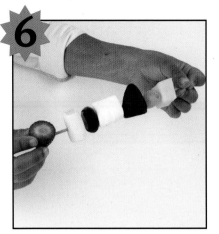

- When the chocolate has melted, take the pan off the heat.
- Turn off the burner.
- Using one of the wooden skewers, dip some of the fruits and marshmallows into the melted chocolate.

- Leave the chocolate-covered fruits and marshmallows on the cooling rack to set.

- Thread the fruit and marshmallows on to the skewers. Push the skewers through the parts not covered in chocolate.

So Good!

| 1 hour |
| Easy |
| Uncooked |

How To!

Crack Open an Egg

1
- Tap the egg gently on the side of a bowl so that it cracks.

2
- Put your two thumbs on either side of the crack.

3
- Hold the egg over the bowl and gently pull the shell apart.

Separate an Egg

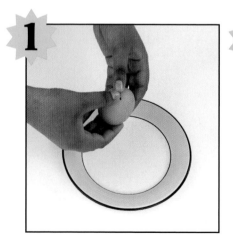

1
- Break the egg on to a plate.

2
- Place an egg cup over the egg yolk.

3
- Hold the egg cup in place and pour the egg white into a bowl.

Grate

A food grater has lots of sharp blades that can turn food into strips.

A box grater has different-sized blades for different foods.

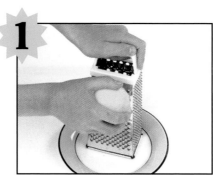

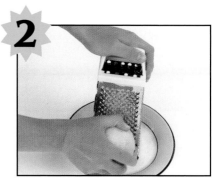

- The finest blades are for grating the rind of oranges and lemons.

- Hold the top of the grater to keep it from slipping.
- Press food against the blades and push down.
- Watch your fingers.

Whisk or Beat

To whisk or beat means to stir quickly to add air to a liquid. Whipping cream is beaten to make it thick.

Beaters and whisks are kitchen utensils designed for stirring liquids quickly (see page 31).

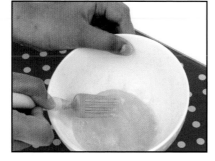

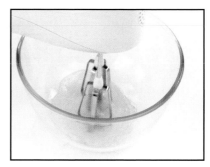

- This egg yolk is being whisked with a fork.

- Beating egg whites is much quicker using an electric mixer.

Mash

A potato masher is used to mash food. It has holes in it that the food is pushed through to break it up.

A fork can be used to mash soft foods such as bananas.

- Potatoes are usually mashed with a potato masher.

- This banana is being mashed with a fork.

Glossary

artificial coloring A manufactured coloring added to food.

artificial flavoring Manufactured flavors that are added to food.

bake To cook in an oven with heat all around the food.

broil A way of cooking food using direct heat from above or below.

energy A type of power that can be used. Food is changed to energy in our body.

exercise Physical activity that uses up calories (energy) and improves fitness.

fat 1. A greasy substance found in food. Fats in food are divided into two types: **saturated fats** are found in cream, cheese, butter, fatty meat, and chocolate; **unsaturated fats** are found in avocados, nuts, vegetable oils, and olive oils. Unsaturated fats are healthier than saturated fats. 2. Tissue in the human body where energy is stored.

fiber The part of a fruit or vegetable that cannot be digested. Fiber helps the digestion of other food.

mineral A substance such as iron or calcium that the body needs to function properly. Minerals are found in foods.

oily fish Fish that have oily flesh. These fish contain substances that help to prevent heart disease.

preservative A substance used to keep food from going bad.

processed food Any food product that has been changed in some way. Cooking, freezing, drying, canning, and preserving are all methods of processing food. Processed foods may contain colorings, flavorings, and other additives and preservatives.

protein A substance found in some foods. It is needed by the body to grow and develop properly. Meat, eggs, milk, and some types of beans contain protein.

starchy Describes a food that contains starch. Starchy foods make up one of the food groups. They include bread, cereals, rice, pasta, and potatoes.

superfine sugar A type of very fine white sugar with small grains.

vegetarian Someone who eats no meat or fish. Some vegetarians do eat dairy foods and eggs.

vitamin One of the substances that are essential in very small amounts in the body for normal growth and activity.

whole grain Cereals such as wheat, barley, and oats that have not had the outer layer taken off.

whole wheat The entire grain of wheat including the outer layer (bran).

Equipment

wire cooling rack

strainer

cutting board

pastry brush

measuring cup

spatula

mixing bowl

grater

mixing or serving spoon

whisk

tablespoon

teaspoon

saucepan

knife

small sharp knife

frying pan

You will also need:
dish towel
oven mitts
tin foil
electric mixer
baking dish
wooden skewers

wooden spoons

colander

non-stick baking sheet

Index

Activity Sheets

Request these free activity sheets at:
info@blackrabbitbooks.com.

Pages 4–5 All about Dinner

Plan your dinner for the week ahead on this handy food chart. Fill in the shopping list so you know what you need to buy.

Pages 6–7 All about Dinner

Which dinner do your friends like best?
Fill in this food survey to find out which are the most popular.

Page 31 Equipment

Download a colorful poster of all the equipment used in the *"Plan, Prepare, Cook"* books.